T0413974

Turkey

LEVEL 5

/ey/

Teaching Tips

Green Level 5

This book focuses on the phoneme **/ey/**.

Before Reading

- Discuss the title. Ask readers what they think the book will be about. Have them briefly explain why.
- Ask readers to look at the pictures and words on page 3. Sound out the words together. What other words end in "ey"?

Read the Book

- Encourage readers to break down unfamiliar words into units of sound. Then, ask them to string the sounds together to create the words.
- Urge readers to point out when the focused phonics phoneme appears in the text.

After Reading

- Encourage children to reread the book independently or with a friend.
- Ask readers to name other words with the /ey/ phoneme. On a separate sheet of paper, have them write the words out.

© 2024 Booklife Publishing
This edition is published by arrangement with Booklife Publishing.

North American adaptations © 2024 Jump!
5357 Penn Avenue South
Minneapolis, MN 55419
www.jumplibrary.com

Decodables by Jump! are published by Jump! Library.

Library of Congress Cataloging-in-Publication Data is available at www.loc.gov or upon request from the publisher.

ISBN: 979-8-88996-846-7 (hardcover)
ISBN: 979-8-88996-847-4 (paperback)
ISBN: 979-8-88996-848-1 (ebook)

Photo Credits

Images are courtesy of Shutterstock.com. With thanks to Getty Images, Thinkstock Photo and iStockphoto. Cover – topseller, Marti Bug Catcher, Carmian. 3 – Rosa Jay, Dionisvera, AlexGreenArt. 4–5 – Seqoya, Prostock–studio. 6–7 – MehmetO, Hakan Tanak. 8–9 – DreamStoreCo, Nick N A. 10–11 – alexfan32, SergeyKPI. 12–13 – Giancarlo Polacchini, Tehsin Baravi. 14–15 – Olena Yakobchuk, frantic00. 16 – Shutterstock.

How many words can you think of that have an **ey** sound? Here are a few to get you started:

Key

Honey

Donkey

The key to a fun trip away is to plan things to see and do as you travel.

Turkey is an interesting spot to travel to. There are some things in Turkey that you must not miss.

Turkey is next to the sea. You can visit a Turkish beach as part of the trip.

Turkey has a lot of high hills, such as Mount Ararat. It has lots of valleys too.

Mount Ararat

If you go to Pasabag Valley, you will see lots of rock chimneys in a cluster.

You might see hot air balloons near the chimneys. You could go in one to survey the chimneys from up high.

When you go, you will need to get Turkish coins. You can spend them at a market.

You can spend the coins on street food too. You can get food, such as hot corn, from red trolleys.

Corn

In Mardin, donkeys help keep the streets clean. They go up thin stairs and alleys that big trucks cannot.

Donkey

They are fed well with food such as barley.

Barley

Turkey has lots of interesting people and spots to visit.

There is too much to see in just one trip.
You will have to go back to see it all!

Trace the /ey/ sound to complete each word. Say the words out loud.

monkey

turkey

hockey